The Missions: California's Heritage

MISSION
SAN FRANCISCO SOLANO

by

Mary Null Boulé

Merryant Publishing
Vashon, Washington

Book Twenty One in a series of twenty-one

With special thanks to Msgr. Francis J. Weber, Archivist of the
Los Angeles Catholic Diocese for his encouragement and expertise
in developing this series.

ISBN: 1-877599-20-4

Father Junípero Serra

INTRODUCTION

Building of a mission church involved everyone in the mission community. Priests were engineers and architects; Native Americans did the construction. Mission Indian in front is pouring adobe mix into a brick form. Bricks were then dried in the sun.

FATHER SERRA AND THE MISSIONS: AN INTRODUCTION

The year was 1769. On the east coast of what would soon become the United States, the thirteen original colonies were making ready to break away from England. On the west coast of our continent, however, there could be found only untamed land inhabited by Native Americans, or Indians. Although European explorers had sailed up and down the coast in their ships, no one but American Indians had explored the length of this land on foot . . . until now.

To this wild, beautiful country came a group of adventurous men from New Spain, as Mexico was then called. They were following the orders of their king, King Charles III of Spain.

One of the men was a Spanish missionary named Fray Junípero Serra. He had been given a tremendous job; especially since he was fifty-six years old, an old man in those days. King Charles III had ordered mission settlements to be built along the coast of Alta (Upper) California and it was Fr. Serra's task to carry out the king's wishes.

Father Serra had been born in the tiny village of Petra

on the island of Mallorca, Spain. He had done such an excellent job of teaching and working with the Indians in Mexican missions, the governor of New Spain had suggested to the king that Fr. Serra do the same with the Indians of Alta California. Hard-working Fray Serra was helped by Don Gaspár de Portolá, newly chosen governor of Alta California, and two other Franciscan priests who had grown up with Fr. Serra in Mallorca, Father Fermín Lasuén and Father Francisco Palóu.

There were several reasons why men had been told to build settlements along the coast of this unexplored country. First, missions would help keep the land as Spanish territory. Spain wanted to be sure the rest of the world knew it owned this rich land. Second, missions were to be built near harbors so towns would grow there. Ships from other countries could then stop to trade with the Spaniards, but these travelers could not try to claim the land for themselves. Third, missions were a good way to turn Indians into Christian, hard-working people.

It would be nice if we could write here that everything went well; that twenty-one missions immediately sprang up along the coast. Unfortunately, all did not go well. It would take fifty-four years to build all the California missions. During those fifty-four years many people died from Indian attacks, sickness, and starvation. Earthquakes and fires constantly ruined mission buildings, which then had to be built all over again. Fr. Serra calmly overcame each problem as it happened, as did those priests who followed him.

When a weary Fray Serra finally died in 1784, he had founded nine missions from San Diego to Monterey and had arranged the building of many more. Fr. Lasuén con-tinued Fr. Serra's work, adding eight more missions to the California mission chain. The remaining four missions were founded in later years.

Originally, plans had been to place missions a hard day's walk from each other. Many of them were really quite far apart. Travelers truly struggled to go from one mission to another along the 650 miles of walking road known as El Camino Real, The Royal Highway. Today keen eyes will sometimes see tall, curved poles with bells hanging from them sitting by the side of streets and highways. These bell poles are marking a part of the old El Camino Real.

At first Spanish soldiers were put in charge of the towns which grew up near each mission. The priests were told to handle only the mission and its properties. It did not take long to realize the soldiers were not kind and gentle leaders. Many were uneducated and did not have the understanding they should have had in dealing with people. So the padres came to be in charge of not only the mission, but of the townspeople and even of the soldiers.

The first missions at San Diego and Monterey were built near the ocean where ships could bring them needed supplies. After early missions began to grow their own food and care for themselves, later mission compounds were built farther away from the coast. What one mission did well, such as leatherworking, candlemaking, or raising cattle, was shared with other missions. As a result, missions became somewhat specialized in certain products.

Although mission buildings looked different from mission to mission, most were built from one basic plan. Usually a compound was constructed as a large, four-sided building with an inner patio in the center. The outside of the quadrangle had only one or two doors, which were locked at night to protect the mission. A church usually sat at one corner of the quadrangle and was always the tallest and largest part of the mission compound.

Facing the inner patio were rooms for the two priests living there, workshops, a kitchen, storage rooms for grain and food, and the mission office. Rooms along the back of the quadrangle often served as home to the unmarried Indian women who worked in the kitchen. The rest of the Indians lived just outside the walls of the mission in their own village.

Beyond the mission wall and next to the church was a cemetery. Today you can still see many of the original headstones of those who died while living and working at the mission. Also outside the walls were larger workshops, a reservoir holding water used at the mission, and orchards containing fruit trees. Huge fields surrounded each mission where crops grew and livestock such as sheep, cattle, and horses grazed.

It took a great deal of time for some Indian tribes to under-stand the new way of life a mission offered, even though the

Native Americans always had food and shelter when they became mission Indians. Each morning all Indians were awakened at sunrise by a church bell calling them to church. Breakfast followed church . . . and then work. The women spun thread and made clothes, as well as cooked meals. Men and older boys worked in workshops or fields and constructed buildings. Meanwhile the Indian children went to school, where the padres taught them. After a noon meal there was a two hour rest before work began again. After dinner the Indians sang, played, or danced. This way of life was an enormous change from the less organized Indian life before the missionaries arrived. Many tribes accepted the change, some had more trouble getting used to a regular schedule, some tribes never became a part of mission life.

Water was all-important to the missions. It was needed to irrigate crops and to provide for the mission people and animals. Priests designed and engineered magnificent irrigation systems at most of the missions. All building of aqueducts and reservoirs of these systems was done by the mission Indians.

With all the organized hard work, the missions did very well. They grew and became strong. Excellent vineyards gave wine for the priests to use and to sell. Mission fields produced large grain crops of wheat and corn, and vast grazing land developed huge herds of cattle and sheep. Mission life was successful for over fifty years.

When Mexico broke away from Spain, it found it did not have enough money to support the California missions, as Spain had been doing. So in 1834, Mexico enforced the secularization law which their government had decreed several years earlier. This law stated missions were to be taken away from the missionaries and given to the Indians. The law said that if an Indian did not want the land or buildings, the property was to be sold to anyone who wished to buy it.

It is true the missions had become quite large and powerful. And as shocked as the padres were to learn of the secularization law, they also knew the missions had originally been planned as temporary, or short term projects. The priests had been sure their Indians would be well-trained enough to run the missions by themselves when the time came to move to other unsettled lands. In fact, however, even after fifty years the California Indians were still not ready to handle the huge missions.

Since the Indians did not wish to continue the missions, the buildings and land were sold, the Indians not even waiting for money or, in some cases, receiving money for the sale.

Sad times lay ahead. Many Indians went back to the old way of life. Some Indians stayed on as servants to the new owners and often these owners were not good to them. Mission buildings were used for everything from stores and saloons to animal barns. In one mission the church became a barracks for the army. A balcony was built for soldiers with their horses stabled in the altar area. Rats ate the stored grain and beautiful church robes. Furniture and objects left by the padres were stolen. People even stole the mission building roof tiles, which then caused the adobe brick walls to melt from rain. Earthquakes finished off many buildings.

Shortly after California became a part of the United States in the mid-1860s, our government returned all mission buildings to the Catholic Church. By this time most of them were in terrible condition. Since the priests needed only the church itself and a few rooms to live in, the other rooms of the mission were rented to anyone who needed them. Strange uses were found in some cases. In the San Fernando Mission, for example, there was once a pig farm in the patio area.

Tourists finally began to notice the mission ruins in the early 1900s. Groups of interested people got together to see if the missions could be restored. Some missions had been "modernized" by this time, unfortunately, but within the last thirty years historians have found enough pictures, drawings, and written descriptions to rebuild or restore most of the missions to their original appearances.

The restoration of all twenty-one missions is a splendid way to preserve our California heritage. It is the hope of many Californians that this dream of restoration can become a reality in the near future.

MISSION SAN FRANCISCO SOLANO

I. THE MISSION TODAY

San Francisco Solano is in the city of Sonoma facing a corner of the historic Sonoma Pueblo Plaza. In fact, the city actually grew up because of the mission. Today, after patient restoration, a small chapel built on the site of the original wood chapel and the monastery, or padre's wing, make up all that is left of the old mission.

The chapel, rebuilt in 1914, is adobe brick and has been plastered inside and out with white plaster. The outside walls are the same size as the original small chapel of 1823, and measure 22 feet wide and 105 feet long. The roof is of tile, replaced in 1913. The dark wood beams above the squared, recessed entrance and window are the only decoration to the front of the church.

The inside walls of the church have been decorated with fresco painting styled after small pieces of wall that were left standing in the old ruin. This kind of decoration was usually the kind Indians used on mission walls, so it is probably quite a bit like what was there originally. The Stations of the Cross hang on the walls. Chandeliers made to look like those of other missions are hung from the beamed ceiling. Many gifts of church items, some from the old church, have been given to furnish the chapel.

The monastery wing is about the same size as the chapel and forms an L to it. This wing contains a small, but growing museum. A corridor covers the front of the padre's wing. It has a tile floor and posts, instead of arches, supporting the tile roof.

In front of the chapel is the second bell used in mission days. The first bell has never been found. This bell has a Spanish style top, even though it was made in Mexico. Once a year the blessing of the grapes takes place in front of the bell.

11

II. HISTORY OF THE MISSION

Mission San Francisco Solano was the 21st, and last, mission built in the California mission chain. One wonders if the mission would have ever been founded at all if it had not been for an ambitious, zealous, young Spanish priest at Mission Dolores in San Francisco. Father José Altimira had a burning desire to develop new missions, baptize Indians by the hundreds, and become the "new" Father Serra.

Fr. Altimira felt trapped at Mission Dolores. Instead of going to the Father-Presidente of the missions about his problems and goals, as was required of all priests, he went to a military friend of his who had recently become governor of California. Fr. Altimira wrote several letters to the governor complaining of the poor farmland around Mission Dolores. He wrote of the illnesses of his natives caused by the foggy, rainy climate of San Francisco.

Actually, Mission San Rafael had already been built in the sunny land north of Mission Dolores, as a hospital for the sick Indians. This made no difference to Fr. Altimira. He wanted his own mission. What is more, he wanted to move both Missions Dolores and San Rafael even further north to a place he had discovered, a site which no one else had seen.

The California governor was delighted at the thought of closing two missions and building only one mission in their place. He felt there were too many missions as it was. He especially liked the thought of a mission so close to Fort Ross, a large Russian settlement along the northern coast of California. Having a mission in that area was a good way to keep an eye on the Russians. For these reasons he encouraged this ambitious priest who wanted to build his own mission.

Fr. Altimira, with only the governor's permission, went north with a small group of men. Selecting the spot for his mission, he had his own founding ceremony on July 4, 1823. Fr. Altimira named it "New San Francisco Mission." In August of that year he returned with eleven Indians and one military man and began to cut logs, put up fences, and dig irrigation ditches.

Of course, he had no church permission to do this. When Father-Presidente Sarria heard of Fr. Altimira's plans a week later, he refused approval of a new mission. The young priest obeyed his superior and stopped work on the buildings, but he was furious. He wrote an angry letter to the governor, complaining of his problems. After many letters between the three men, a compromise was reached. Mission Dolores and San Rafael were to stay where they were. . .San Rafael was to become a full mission and Fr. Altimira was allowed to continue building on his mission. However, the mission was to be named San Francisco Solano for St. Francis Solano, a missionary to the Indies and Peru, instead of being named the "New San Francisco de Asis."

Father Altimira returned to the mission site in October of 1823, finishing the buildings he had begun earlier. He laid out brickyards for the making of adobe brick, built kilns, and started the foundations for the church. The first year's records show 482 Native Americans in the mission, although many of those were from Mission Dolores and Mission San Rafael. By 1825, he had finished the priest's house, a granary, and thatched houses for the guards. In 1826, the adobe wall around the quadrangle was built with tile on top of the adobe. More Indians were arriving. The weaving rooms were now finished so cloth was being made for the mission by the Indian women. Tiles were being made by the thousands for floors and roofs.

Then, in 1827, some Indian troublemakers became restless and began setting fire to some of the buildings and supplies. It was beginning to come clear that Fr. Altimira may have had much ambition, but he did not know how to get along with people. He was so discouraged by the troubles with the Indians, even though other missions had had the same problems at first, that he simply left this mission he had wanted so badly, finally arriving at San Buenaventura Mission. In January of 1828, Fr. Altimira left for Spain without asking permission or telling his superiors he was leaving.

Father Buenaventura Fortuny took Fr. Altimira's place at Mission Solano. He found the mission Indians confused and disorganized from Fr. Altimira's treatment of them. However, Fr. Fortuny was an excellent priest and leader. Within two years he had the mission running better than ever.

In 1827 foundations were laid for a large new adobe church. It took five years to build. When Fr. Fortuny retired the year

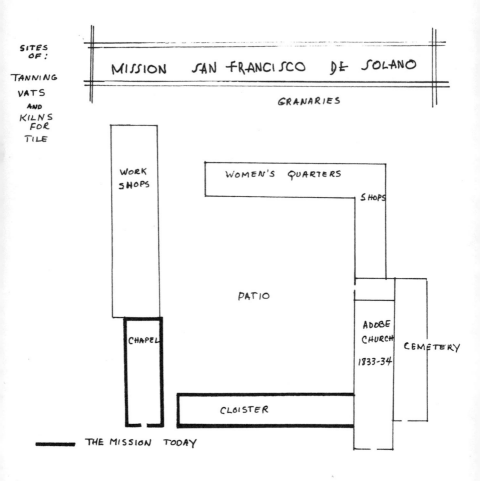

SITES
OF:

TANNING
VATS
AND
KILNS
FOR
TILE

MISSION   SAN FRANCISCO   DE SOLANO

GRANARIES

WORK SHOPS

WOMEN'S QUARTERS

SHOPS

PATIO

CHAPEL

ADOBE CHURCH 1833-34

CEMETERY

CLOISTER

━━━ THE MISSION TODAY

the large church was dedicated, he had enlarged the mission to thirty buildings. This was also the year that Mexico broke away from Spain, so there were many Mexican priests who came and went in the two years after Fr. Fortuny left. Then secularization came in 1834.

During all the years the mission was active, a Mexican general, Mariano Vallejo, had been in charge of the military men and the city of Sonoma. His job was to keep the Russians out of the area and to see that the town was built up with Mexican settlers. He had become very powerful, but had always been kind to the mission and its priests. He had even paid for the restoring of the small mission chapel at one time. The large adobe church had proved to be far too large for the town to use. The townspeople had always preferred the small chapel on the corner by the plaza.

Now, with secularization, General Vallejo took over the managing of the mission's property. He gave the smaller items around the mission to the Indians as he was supposed to do by law, but the Indians did not know what to do with them. So he took them back and took the mission's farmlands as well. He sold some of the mission's land to his relatives and became quite wealthy. He used the mission Indians as servants at his home.

Settlers used the mission's tiles and wood beams for the building of their own houses. Unfortunately, when tile is removed from the top of adobe brick it melts down into mud again when it rains. By 1839 the mission was in ruins.

In 1846, one of the most exciting events in California's history happened right across from the newly restored mission chapel. A group of American settlers had become disturbed with Mexico's way of ruling their property. They organized a government called the California Republic and chose the Sonoma Plaza flagpole to raise their new flag proclaiming California a free republic. The flag has a red star and a brown bear on a white background. A wide red band was along the bottom of it. It looked a great deal like the California state flag does today. The settlers then took over the town of Sonoma and put General Vallejo in jail. Before any real trouble started, however, the United States Marines landed in Monterey and the war between Mexico and the U.S. for the possession of California had begun.

Because of the war, California's new statehood, and the new Catholic church built across town from the mission, no one really cared any longer what happened to Mission Solano. It was sold to a man who built a saloon right in front of the mission chapel entrance. He stored his liquor and hay in the chapel.

It took the interest of the Historic Landmark League to save the few walls left standing of poor Mission San Francisco Solano. In 1903 this group bought the property upon which the chapel and the padre's wing sat. Slowly they began to restore and repair the ruins. An earthquake in 1912 interrupted the work, but the League simply began all over again. In 1926 the League gave the partly restored mission to the state. Today it is known as Sonoma Mission State Historic Park and is cared for by the state. With the help and concern of many people, the mission which was so much a part of early California statehood is once more taking its proper place in California history.

Interior view of present chapel replica at Solano. Fresco painting on walls is done in colors used by Native Americans in mission days. Tall pulpit on right is where priest stood to speak to those attending church services

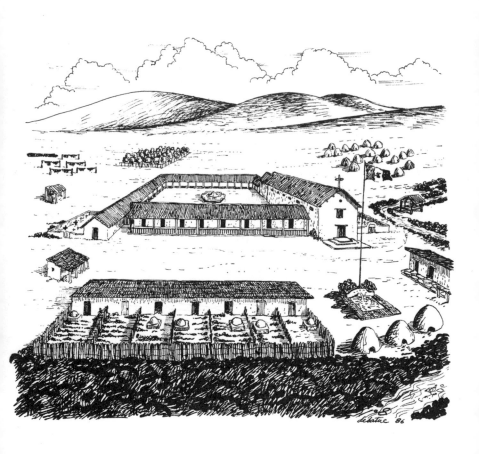

Artist concept of mission quadrangle during 1830s.

OUTLINE OF MISSION SAN FRANCISCO SOLANO

I. The mission today

   A. Location
   B. Chapel exterior
      1. Walls
      2. Size of chapel
   C. Chapel interior
      1. Fresco painted walls
      2. Stations of the Cross
      3. Gifts donated to decorate chapel
   D. Monastery wing
      1. Museum
      2. Arcade description
      3. Tile roof
   E. Bell

II. History of the mission

   A. Father José Altimira
      1. Goals and ambition
      2. Unhappiness at Mission Dolores
      3. Founding of San Francisco Solano without permission
      4. The compromise
   B. The growth of the mission
      1. Building of brickyard, kilns, church, etc.
   C. Fr. Altimira leaves
      1. Fr. Fortuny arrives
         a. New large church
         b. Thirty buildings
         c. Fr. Fortuny retires, 1832
   D. General Vallejo
      1. Makes money off sale of mission land
   E. Secularization
   F. California Republic
      1. Bear flag on Plaza flagpole
      2. General Vallejo jailed
   G. Ruin of mission
   H. Restoration
      1. Historic Landmark League 1903 and becoming state park.

GLOSSARY

BUTTRESS: a large mass of stone or wood used to strengthen buildings

CAMPANARIO: a wall which holds bells

CLOISTER: an enclosed area; a word often used instead of convento

CONVENTO: mission building where priests lived

CORRIDOR: covered, outside hallway found at most missions

EL CAMINO REAL: highway between missions; also known as The King's Highway

FACADE: front wall of a building

FONT: large, often decorated bowl containing Holy Water for baptizing people

FOUNDATION: base of a building, part of which is below the ground

FRESCO: designs painted directly on walls or ceilings

LEGEND: a story coming from the past

PORTICO: porch or covered outside hallway

PRESERVE: to keep in good condition without change

PRESIDIO: a settlement of military men

QUADRANGLE: four-sided shape; the shape of most missions

RANCHOS: large ranches often many miles from mission proper where crops were grown and animal herds grazed

REBUILD: to build again; to repair a great deal of something

REPLICA: a close copy of the original

REREDOS: the wall behind the main altar inside the church

*RESTORATION: to bring something back to its original condition (see * below)

SANCTUARY: area inside, at the front of the church where the main altar is found

SECULARIZATION: something not religious; a law in mission days taking the mission buildings away from the church and placing them under government rule

*ORIGINAL: the first one; the first one built

BIBLIOGRAPHY

Bauer, Helen, *California Mission Days.* Sacramento, CA: California State Department of Education, 1957.

Goodman, Marian. *Missions of California.* Redwood City, CA: Redwood City Tribune, 1961

Smilie, Robert S. *The Sonoma Mission.* Fresno, CA 93721: Valley Publishers, 1975.

Sunset Editors. *The California Missions.* Menlo Park, CA: Lane Publishing Co., 1979.

Wright, Ralph B., ed. *California Missions.* Arroyo Grande, CA 93420: Hubert A. Lowman, 1977.

For more information about this mission, write to:

> Mission San Francisco Solano
> Sonoma, CA 93570

It is best to enclose a self-addressed, stamped envelope and a small amount of money to pay for brochures and pictures the mission might send you.

Acknowledgement
Chris Stokes, Ranger

CREDITS

Cover art and Father Serra Illustration: Ellen Grim
Illustrations: Alfredo de Batuc
Ground Layout: Mary Boulé